For the Love of the Cardinals

An A–Z Primer for Cardinal Fans of All Ages

Foreword by Ozzie Smith

Written by Frederick C. Klein

Illustrated by Mark Anderson

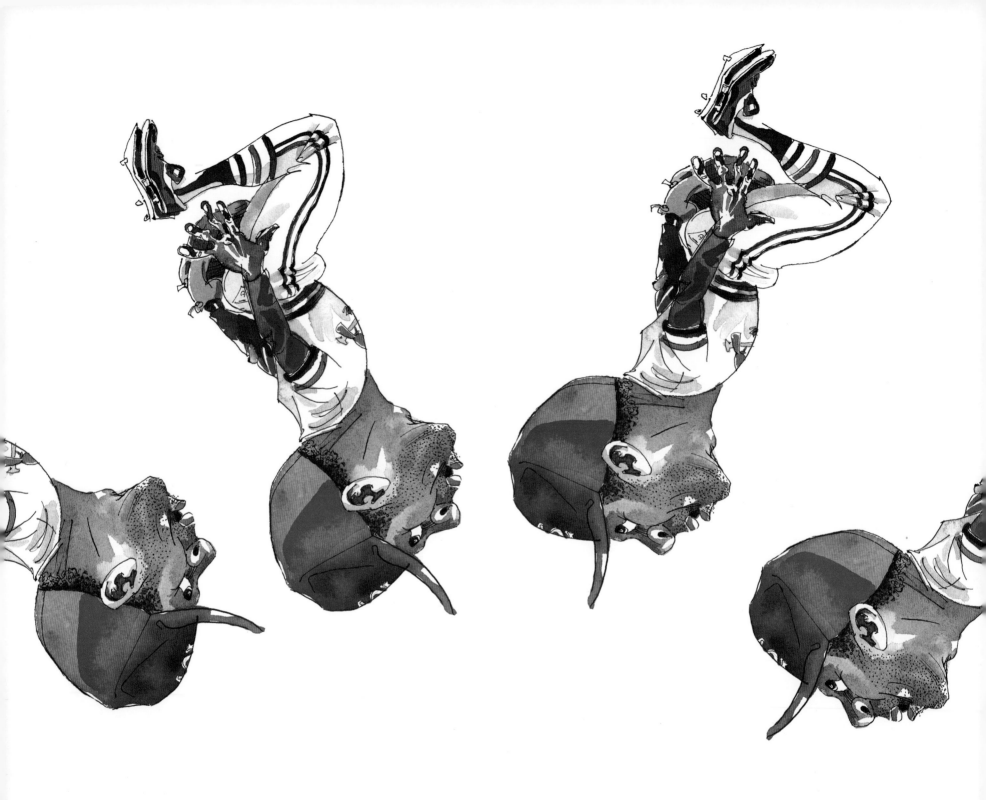

Foreword

Playing Major League Baseball is a dream that all children have when they are growing up. I was one of the lucky ones whose dreams came true. Never for one day did I fail to realize how lucky and privileged I was.

Playing for the St. Louis Cardinals allowed me to achieve even more than I could have dreamed. Wearing the uniform with the "Birds on the Bat" logo across my chest for 15 years gave me an understanding and appreciation for the love that people have for the Cardinals.

That love begins at a young age and is passed down from generation to generation, from fathers to sons and from mothers to daughters. Everybody who goes to a game at Busch Stadium and cheers for Albert Pujols and his teammates hears stories about Stan Musial, Red Schoendienst, Bob Gibson, Lou Brock, and now even Ozzie Smith. It is part of what makes baseball such a great game and the Cardinals such a special team.

Youngsters reading this book, or having it read to them by their parents, will quickly begin to understand why I was so proud to wear a Cardinals uniform. Somebody reading this book will no doubt dream about becoming the next Cardinals great, and I really hope those dreams come true as they did for me.

Ozzie Smith

A is for Alexander,

Whose bag of mound tricks
Stopped the mighty Yankees
In nineteen twenty-six.

Grover Cleveland Alexander was one of baseball's greatest pitchers, a right-hander whose 373 victories over 20 major league seasons rank third on the all-time list. Most of those wins were with the Philadelphia Phillies or Chicago Cubs, but some of his finest moments came with the Cardinals, whom he joined in 1926 at the advanced baseball age of 39. With his help the Cards won their first National League pennant that year and faced the Babe Ruth–led New York Yankees in the World Series. Alexander won Games 2 and 6 of the Series with complete-game performances, and despite having pitched the day before, he entered Game 7 in New York in the seventh inning with the Cards ahead, 3–2. With the bases loaded and two out, he struck out Tony Lazzeri to end that threat, then set down the Yanks in the final two innings to preserve the victory and secure the title for his team.

B is for Brock,

Larceny was his game.
Stolen-base prowess
Was his ticket to fame.

Lou Brock came to the Cardinals from the Cubs in a 1964 trade for Ernie Broglio, a starting pitcher whose career soon went into decline. The transaction turned out so well for St. Louis that "Brock-for-Broglio" became baseball shorthand for a one-sided deal. The speedy Brock became a 16-season starter in left field for the Cards, collecting 3,023 career hits and 938 stolen bases, the latter figure a major league record at the time of his retirement in 1979. Many of his steals came on the headfirst slides that were his trademark.

C is for Carlton and Carpenter,

One lefty, one right.
With them on the hill
Cards' prospects were bright.

Steve Carlton was a left-handed pitcher who spent the first seven of his 24 big-league seasons with the Cards. His great fastball and wicked slider enabled him to post 329 career victories, the second most ever for a lefty, and his 4,136 strikeouts rank fourth all-time. **Chris Carpenter**, **who throws right-handed**, **has been the Cards' pitching ace for the last four seasons**. The 6'5" native of New Hampshire won the National League Cy Young Award in 2005 with a 21–5 won-lost record. In 2006 he won 15 regular-season games and three more in a postseason from which the Cards emerged with their 10th World Series championship.

D is for
Dean,
Dizzy and Paul.
For the Cards in the '30s,
They did it all.

For two sizzling seasons (1934 and 1935) the brothers Dizzy and Paul Dean, from rural Arkansas, were baseball's most potent pitching combination, winning a total of 96 games for the Cards. Paul, the younger brother, posted 19 wins in each of the two campaigns before injuries cut short his career. Dizzy, so called for his off-center personality (his real first names were Jay Hanna), won 30 games for the 1934 champions and 28 in 1935. Later, he too was hampered by injuries but not before he had recorded Hall of Fame credentials. When his playing days ended Dizzy became a baseball broadcaster known for mangling the English language. That was no matter, he said, noting, "A lot of people who ain't saying ain't, ain't eatin'."

E is for Edmonds,

Who covers lots of ground.
With a glove on his hand
He's the best man around.

Jim Edmonds came to the Cardinals from the Anaheim Angels in a trade before the 2000 season. A swift runner with a flair for making over-the-shoulder catches, he quickly established himself as the National League's best center fielder and went on to win six straight Gold Gloves at the position. He's handy with a bat, too, as attested by his .289 lifetime average and 350 career home runs through 2006.

F is for Flood,

Who stood tall for a cause.
When the players gained freedom
He earned their applause.

Curt Flood was a solid center fielder with the Cardinals for 12 seasons (1958–1969) but made his most memorable mark with an off-field act. When he was traded to the Philadelphia Phillies **in late 1969 he refused to report, instead suing to overturn professional baseball's long-time reserve clause**, which bound players to their teams until the teams chose to trade or release them. He lost in the courts and forfeited playing the 1970 season, but his stand paved the way for a 1975 arbitrator's ruling that struck down the clause and opened the era of free agency that has caused players' salaries to soar.

G is for Gibson,

An intimidating fellow.
He made hitters' knees shake
And their bats turn to Jell-O.

Bob Gibson is considered the Cardinals' best pitcher ever as a result of a 17-season career with the team in which he won 251 games. An excellent athlete who once played with basketball's Harlem Globetrotters, he also was a ferocious competitor who stared down batters from the mound and sent brush-back pitches their way if they dared to crowd the plate. He was at his best in big games. He started three times in each of the three World Series in which he played (1964, 1967, and 1968) and completed eight games, posting a 7–2 won-lost record and an earned-run average of 1.89. His three complete-game victories in the 1967 Series against the Boston Red Sox was the main factor in the Cards' seven-game triumph.

H is for

Hornsby;

His vision was fine.
He battered the pitchers
Like rugs on a line.

Rogers Hornsby played in the majors for 23 seasons and had a lifetime batting average of .358, the highest of any right-handed hitter and the second highest of any player, behind only Ty Cobb's .367. Hornsby was a great believer in physical fitness and went so far as to refuse to see movies or read books for fear it would harm his batting eye. His most productive years were in St. Louis, where he hit a colossal .424 in one season (1924) and over .400 in two others. The second baseman became the Cards' player/manager in 1925 and the next year led the club to its first National League pennant and World Series crown.

I is for Isringhausen,

The Cards' fire chief.
He's better than Tums
When it comes to relief.

The Cardinals have had relief-pitching aces such as Dennis Eckersley, Bruce Sutter, and Lee Smith, but **the team record for saves—173 through 2006—is held by Jason Isringhausen**. A native of Brighton, Illinois, just north of St. Louis, the husky right-hander signed with the Cards as a free agent after the 2001 season and has been the team's top closer every year since. That distinction held in 2006 despite the fact that his season ended in September due to hip surgery. His absence from the playoffs made his team's success there all the more remarkable.

J is for Jack Buck,

Whose voice on the air
Meant the Cardinals were playing
A ballgame somewhere.

John Francis Buck was the Cardinals' broadcaster on station KMOX from 1954 through 2001, first teaming with the legendary Harry Caray and later with Mike Shannon and then his son, Joe Buck. He gained additional acclaim from his national broadcasts of football games and other sporting events. Buck's raspy voice and signature line of "That's a winner!" after Cardinal victories endeared him to the team's fans. After his death in 2002, more than 10,000 people attended a memorial service at Busch Stadium.

K is for

Kaat;

This kitty could scratch.
For hitters in both leagues
He was more than a match.

Jim Kaat, a right-handed pitcher, had a 25-season major league career that touched four decades (1959–1983). In that span **he won 283 games and 16 Gold Gloves**, and made three All-Star Game appearances. His best years were spent in the American League with the Minnesota Twins, but he was still effective in the four seasons with the Cardinals that ended his playing days. He was a spot starter and reliever for the Cards' 1982 champions, appearing in four of the seven games in that year's World Series against the Milwaukee Brewers.

L is for LaRussa,

Who drives the Cards' train.
You can't put much past
This keen baseball brain.

Tony LaRussa became the Cardinals' manager in 1996 after managing the Chicago White Sox and Oakland Athletics for a total of 17 American League seasons. In his first 11 years in St. Louis he led the team into the postseason seven times, winning two National League pennants (2004 and 2006) and one World Series title (2006). He'd previously won the World Series with the 1989 A's. LaRussa is known for his steady leadership and ability to get the most from his players. **At the end of 2006 he led all active major league managers in career victories with 2,297.** He was third all-time in that category, trailing only Connie Mack and John McGraw.

M is for Musial and McGwire,

Whose bats had some pop.
In their eras they led
The Cards to the top.

Stan "The Man" Musial was the greatest Cardinals batsman and one of the team's most popular players. In a 22-season career, all with the Cards, the left-handed hitter sprang from his peculiar, coiled stance to collect 3,630 hits—the fourth most ever—and compile a .331 lifetime batting average. He is the all-time team leader in just about every offensive category and starred on the world championship teams of 1942, 1943, and 1946. **Mark McGwire**, huge and muscular, joined the Cards in 1997 and hit 220 of his 583 career home runs with the team before retiring after the 2001 season. His 70 home runs in 1998 electrified baseball and shattered Roger Maris's previous record of 61, which had stood for 37 years. McGwire led the Cards into the playoffs in 2000 and 2001.

N is for the year
1934,

When the Gas House Gang
Won the title with a roar.

The 1934 Cardinals, nicknamed the Gas House Gang, were one of baseball's most colorful ensembles, a raucous, brawling group whose antics helped dispel the gloom caused by the national economic depression. Led by Rogers Hornsby, Frankie Frisch, Joe "Ducky" Medwick, Pepper Martin, and Dizzy and Paul Dean, the Gang edged out the New York Giants for the National League pennant on the season's last weekend and won the World Series from the Detroit Tigers. The seventh game of that Series had to be halted when a fight, started by a high-spikes slide into third base by Medwick, incited Detroit fans to throw garbage at him when he took his left-field position in the next inning. Medwick had to be removed from the game but the Cards won anyway, 11–0.

Ozzie Smith was the Cardinals' shortstop from 1982 through 1996 and gained recognition as perhaps the best ever to play his demanding position. He distinguished himself statistically by setting career records for assists (8,375) and double plays (1,590) among shortstops, but his great range and diving, often acrobatic, catches created a more vivid impression. Sometimes, to celebrate an important victory, he'd do a back flip on the field.

O is for Ozzie;

This Smith was a wiz.
He made playing shortstop
A form of showbiz.

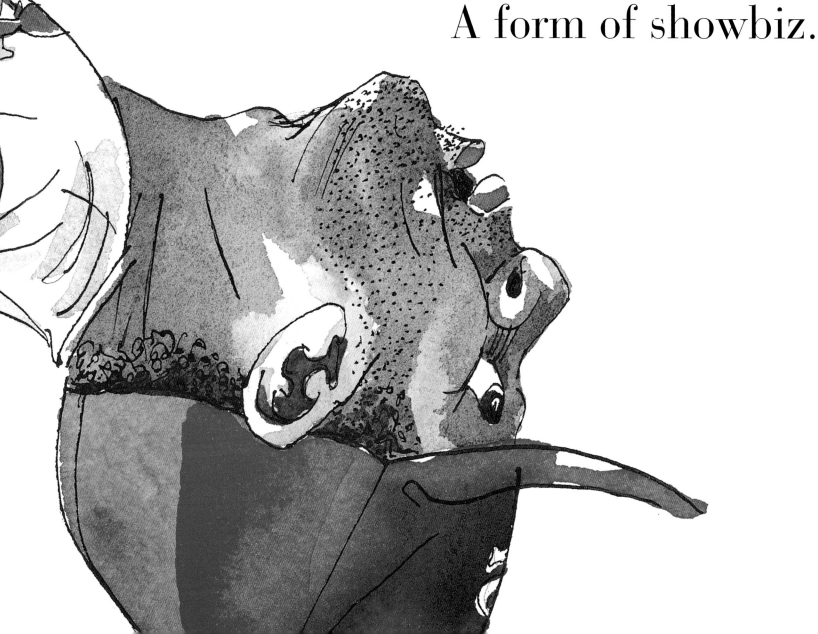

P is for Pujols,

A man with big clout.
Foes can't find a way
To get the guy out.

Albert Pujols, from the Dominican Republic, is baseball's best young hitter, a player who possesses a rare blend of power and ability to make contact with the ball that could, in time, rewrite many all-time records. Pujols joined the Cards in 2001 at age 21 and won the National League Rookie of the Year award with a .329 batting average, 37 home runs, and 130 runs batted in that year. Through 2006, his career batting mark stood at .332 and he had averaged 42 homers and 126 RBIs annually. The first baseman was voted his league's Most Valuable Player after the 2005 season and was runner-up for the award in 2006.

Q is for Quisenberry,

A pitcher of note.
The ball he threw looked like
It came off a U-boat.

Dan Quisenberry was what's known as a "submariner," a pitcher whose ground-scraping, up-from-under throwing motion is strange to look at but has baffled batters since the beginning of baseball time. He had his best years in the American League with the Kansas City Royals, and starred in relief on the Royals team that defeated the Cardinals in the 1985 World Series, but he later spent two seasons in St. Louis. "Quiz" also was quick with a quip. Said he of his unusual style: "I found a delivery in my flaw."

R is for Red Schoendienst,

A bright star at second.
He took up the reins when
Opportunity beckoned.

No name appears more often in Cardinals history than that of Albert "Red" Schoendienst.
The lean second baseman came up with the team in 1945 and spent 15 of his 19 major league seasons with it, many of them highlighted by All-Star Game appearances. After his retirement he became a Cards coach and was named their manager in 1965. He served 12 years in that job, guiding the 1967 World Series champions and winning another National League pennant the next season. He left St. Louis for a time, then returned as a coach who twice filled in as an interim manager. Counting stints in front-office positions, he spent more than 45 years with the team.

S is for Slaughter,

Whose first-to-home dash
     Made St. Louis hearts glad
And Boston's hopes crash.

Enos "Country" Slaughter, a native of North Carolina known for his hustling play, was a fixture in the Cardinals outfield from 1938 through 1953, except for three years of World War II military service. His greatest moment came in Game 7 of the 1946 World Series against the Boston Red Sox. With the score 3–3 he led off the eighth inning with a single but stayed on first base as the next two batters were retired. Then, with Harry Walker at the plate, he took off to steal second base. Walker stroked a soft hit to left-center field and Slaughter kept running, beating shortstop Johnny Pesky's relay throw to the plate. The run stood up through the ninth inning and the Cards again were champs.

T is for  third base,

Where the Cards have been golden
With Kurowski, Ken Boyer,
And, now, with Scott Rolen.

George "Whitey" Kurowski was the Cardinals' third baseman throughout their 1940s pennant runs. He was a four-time All-Star whose most memorable hit was a home run that won Game 5 of the 1942 World Series against the New York Yankees. **Boyer** manned the position with distinction from 1955 through 1965; he was the National League's Most Valuable Player in 1964. **Rolen, the current occupant of the post, is a seven-time Gold Glover** who hits for both power and average. He's been a solid complement to Albert Pujols in the Cards' batting order.

U is for

Uecker —

Not much of a batter,
But fans came to love
His cute baseball patter.

Bob Uecker spent six big-league seasons as a backup catcher, including two (1964 and 1965) with the Cardinals. His lifetime batting average was a puny .200. After he quit playing, however, he returned to his hometown of Milwaukee, Wisconsin, became the Brewers' radio voice and gained fame for his humor and loud sports jackets. He's also an actor, having played a continuing role in the TV series *Mr. Belvedere* and the radio announcer in the comedy movie *Major League*. **In 2003 he won the Ford C. Frick Award, putting his name in the broadcasters' section of the National Baseball Hall of Fame.**

V is for victory,

And the Cards have been blessed.
Ten World Series titles
Fill a large trophy chest.

The Cardinals won 8,984 games from their founding in 1892 through 2006. They have won 17 pennants, and their 10 World Series crowns (1926, 1931, 1934, 1942, 1944, 1946, 1964, 1967, 1982, and 2006) are the most of any National League team.

W is for White,

Who won many a prize,
Then donned coat and tie
And continued to rise.

Bill White starred at first base for the Cardinals from 1959 through 1965, a period during which he was selected to play in five All-Star Games and won a World Series ring in 1964. He was an excellent fielder and tough-out clutch hitter, and he gained a reputation for being levelheaded and plainspeaking. When his playing days ended he became a broadcaster for the New York Yankees. From 1989 through 1993 he was president of the National League and the highest-ranking African American in professional sports administration.

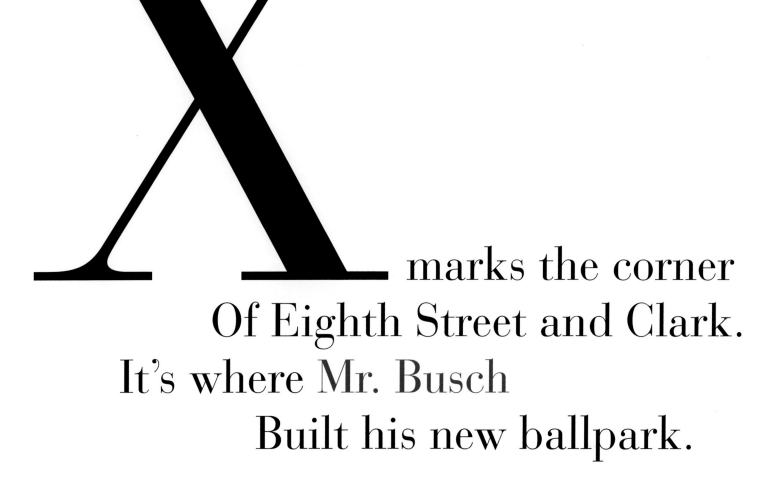

X marks the corner
Of Eighth Street and Clark.
It's where Mr. Busch
Built his new ballpark.

The Cardinals' first home was Robison Field. In 1920 they moved to Sportsman's Park, which they shared with the St. Louis Browns of the American League until that team left for Baltimore in 1953. By the early 1960s Cards owner August A. Busch Jr. decided that a grander domicile was needed and built Busch Stadium, which opened in 1966 at the corner of Eighth and Clark in downtown St. Louis. The team packed 'em into that facility, with season attendance often topping the 3 million mark. Nevertheless, the Busch family wanted a more deluxe facility and built it on a site next to the former field. New Busch Stadium opened in April 2006.

Y is for Young,

His win total is why
The award for best pitcher
Is nicknamed "the Cy."

Denton "Cy" Young was a right-handed pitcher whose 511 career wins, over a 22-season career (1890–1911), set a major league record that is unlikely to be broken. Two of those seasons were with the Cardinals and he led the team in victories in each (26 in 1899, 19 in 1900). A big man and hard thrower, he played in an era in which starting pitchers commonly threw 40 or more complete games in a year and thus posted lots of wins and losses.

"Z" is the sound
Someone makes when he snoozes.
Cards fans stay loyal
Even when their team loses.

— The End

"A" is for Alexander

"B" is for Brock

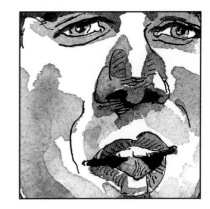

"C" is for Carpenter

"C" is also for Carlton

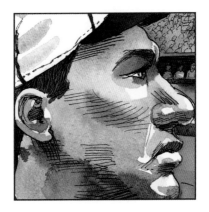

"D" is for Dizzy Dean

"D" is also for Paul Dean

"E" is for Edmonds

"G" is for Gibson

"I" is for Isringhausen

"L" is for LaRussa

"M" is for McGwire

"M" is also for Musial

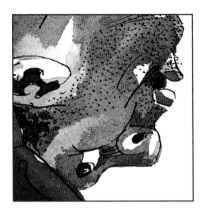

"O" is for Ozzie

"P" is for Pujols

"R" is for Rolen

"S" is for Slaughter

"X" marks the new spot
of the new Busch Stadium

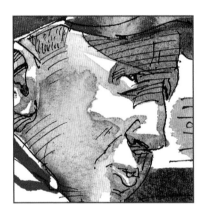

"Y" is for Young

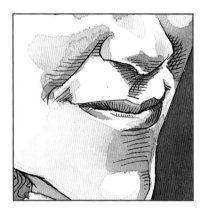

"A" is for Artist

"W" is for Writer

The Cardinals have won 17 pennants, and their 10 World Series crowns
are the most for any National League team.

1926, 1931, 1934, 1942, 1944, 1946, 1964,
1967, 1982, and 2006